The Forbidden City

Author: Susie Hodge

WORLD ALMANAC® LIBRARY

Please visit our web site at: www.worldalmanaclibrary.com
For a free color catalog describing World Almanac® Library's list
of high-quality books and multimedia programs, call 1-800-848-2928 (USA)
or 1-800-387-3178 (Canada). World Almanac® Library's fax: (414) 332-3567.

Library of Congress Cataloging-in-Publication Data

Hodge, Susie, 1960-
  The Forbidden City / by Susie Hodge.
    p. cm. — (Places in history)
  Includes index.
  ISBN 0-8368-5810-7 (lib. bdg.)
  ISBN 0-8368-5817-4 (softcover)
  1. Forbidden City (Beijing, China)—Juvenile literature. 2. Palaces—
China—Beijing—Juvenile literature. I. Title. II. Series.
DS795.8F67H63   2005
951'.156—dc22   2004056925

First published in 2005 by
World Almanac® Library
330 West Olive Street, Suite 100
Milwaukee, WI 53212 USA

This U.S. edition copyright © 2005 by World Almanac® Library. Original edition copyright © 2004
ticktock Entertainment Ltd. First published in Great Britain in 2004 by ticktock Media Ltd.,
Unit 2, Orchard Business Centre, North Farm Road, Tunbridge Wells, Kent, TN2 3XF.

Consultant: Emma Reisz

Photo credits: AA World Travel Library: 2–3, 4L; Associated Press: 39B, 40, 41L, 44L, 45R; Art Archive: 6L, 10, 11L, 12L,
13B, 14L, 14R, 16–17, 27R, 31L, 32L, 33R, 36L, 37R; Bridgeman Art Library: 6–7, 11R, 15, 20B, 21B, 26L, 26–27, 28–29,
31R, 32–33; Corbis: 4–5, 7R, 9T, 16L, 17R, 18T, 18B, 19T, 20–21, 21R, 22L, 22R, 23B, 24L, 24–25, 25BL, 25R, 28, 29R, 30,
34, 35B, 36–37, 38–39, 39T, 41R, 43R, 44–45; Getty Images: 35T; Heritage Images: 5R; Reuters: 42L, 42–43; Robert
Harding Picture Library: 18–19; Werner Forman Archives: 8L, 9B, 12–13, 23T

Printed in the United States of America

1 2 3 4 5 6 7 8 9 09 08 07 06 05

Contents

Introduction

Deep in the center of Beijing, in northern China, and hidden behind a giant wall, is a huge cluster of exotic palaces known as the Forbidden City. The City has also been called Gu Gong, which means "Imperial Palace" in Chinese, and Danei, which means the "Great Within." Between 1420 and 1924, it was home to twenty-four emperors . The Chinese people believed their emperors were chosen by God, and few people, therefore, questioned the emperors' authority. Even today—without any emperors living in it—the Forbidden City looks breathtakingly lavish.

Two bronze lion sculptures flank the entrance to one of the buildings of the Forbidden City. Lions were symbolically regarded as guardians by the Chinese.

Enormous, but Secret

Although no longer occupied by royalty, the Forbidden City remains a symbol of Chinese power and one of the greatest royal palaces in the world. It is made up of nearly one hundred buildings, including magnificent halls, libraries, theaters, temples, homes, storehouses, offices, courtyards, and gardens. It covers about 183 acres (74 hectares) and is surrounded by 33-foot (10-meter) high walls and a 20-foot (6-meter) deep moat.

There are four unique and delicately structured corner towers overlooking the city. Generally, the city was divided into two parts: the northern half, or the Outer Court, where emperors executed their supreme power over the nation, and the southern half, or the Inner Court, where they lived with their royal family. It is thought that it took about one million laborers and craftsmen to build it. From the beginning, it was called the Forbidden City because only the emperor and his family, their staff, and those on official imperial business could enter—ordinary people were not allowed inside. Even ministers and most servants who worked there had only a limited knowledge of its layout as few people could go to all areas of the Forbidden City, even if they lived in it. The main gate, called the Gate of Great Purity, was only opened for an emperor or empress, and many other parts, including paths, steps, and some rooms, were only for the emperor or empress to use. In this way, the city was kept secret from the people for 500 years.

Today, the Forbidden City is the Palace Museum. It contains many works of art and treasures.

From Private to Public

Even though the majority of people living in China were poor, most thought that it was fair for the emperor to live in such luxury. This was because they believed that the emperor was the Son of Heaven, appointed by God to look after the people on Earth. The sumptuous Forbidden City was, therefore, considered the perfect location for a god on Earth to live. Today, the Forbidden City is a popular tourist destination—visited as much for its unique architectural styles and brilliant colors as for the museum full of treasures that currently lies within its great halls. It wasn't until 1925 that the Forbidden City was reincarnated as the Imperial Palace Museum. Many of the beautiful porcelain, jade, ivory, silk, and precious-metal treasures on display at the museum are wartime loot or gifts that arrived in the Forbidden City when it was still an emperor's home. It is appropriate, then, that they should be on display today in the very same location.

The Forbidden City is surrounded by a moat that is known as the Imperial River or the Outer Golden Water River.

The construction of the Forbidden City began in 1406, in the fourth year of Emperor Yongle's reign, and took fourteen years to complete. Astronomers planned the city to align with the North Star, which they believed to be at the center of heaven. Architects planned the Emperor's home to meet all the conditions of feng shui, a set of beliefs about how to work with forces of nature.

A House Fit for a Leader

Emperor Yongle employed two chief workers—Chen Gui, who was in charge of construction, and Wu Zhong, who was in charge of planning. It is commonly believed that one

million workers were forced by the emperor's guards to build the City. Other tradesmen of slightly lesser importance were Lu Xiang (mason), Yang Qing (tiler), and Cai Xin (project manager). Although they might have been named for their involvement, architects and craftspeople did not receive much recognition for their work. They were thought of as mere servants of the emperor.

Materials, such as tiles, wood, and marble, were brought in from across China and shipped to Beijing using the network of canals that were built in the 6th and 7th centuries. Stone came from Fangshang county; marble and square paving tiles came

from Xuzhou; wood came from Sichuan, Guangdong, and Yunnan; colored stones came from Jixian county; granite from Quyang county; and roof tiles from western Beijing. Bricks came from Linqing and were made from a mixture of white lime and glutinous rice, while cement was made from glutinous

Emperor Yongle was the founder of the Ming dynasty (1368–1644). It was he who built the magnificent Forbidden City, located at the heart of the new capital, Beijing.

A dynasty is a succession of rulers who share the same ancestor. A new dynasty can only come to power through the overthrowing of a previous dynasty. From the 3rd century B.C. to the early 20th century, China had twelve major dynastic periods. The first prehistoric dynasty is believed to be Xia, which is thought to have lasted from about the 21st to the 16th century B.C. The two dynasties that resided in the Forbidden City that stands today were the Ming (1368–1644) and Qing (1644–1912).

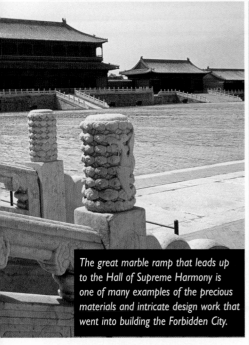

The great marble ramp that leads up to the Hall of Supreme Harmony is one of many examples of the precious materials and intricate design work that went into building the Forbidden City.

rice mixed with egg whites. Amazingly, this mixture made the bricks extremely strong, although light. Massive stones were also used in some of the construction, such as the paths and courtyards. To move these from the canal to the city, workers dug a well every 164 feet (50 m) along the road. In the winter, they poured water from the wells onto the road. When the water turned to ice, they could slide the stones along the road and into the city.

The Forbidden City was built within an enormous rectangle measuring 3,150 feet (960 m) by 2,460 feet (750 m). The outer wall is 33 feet (10 m) high and 28 feet (8.6 m) wide at the base, narrowing at the top to prevent anyone from climbing it. There are only four gateways in this wall and a 171-foot (52-m) wide moat around it. Inside are about 75 buildings with 9,999 rooms (nine is a lucky number in Chinese culture).

Planning and Construction

Like all Chinese monuments, the Forbidden City is built to benefit from good yin-and-yang effects. This is in accordance with feng shui, an important element of Chinese spiritual belief that centers around what it considers the opposite forces in nature. Yin is the feminine and cool force, while yang is the masculine and hot force. During the Ming and Qing periods, feng shui was known only to the astronomers and scientists whose jobs were to maintain the health, wealth, and power of the court.

The Chinese were not interested in building enduring monuments or impressive palaces like those built for European royalty. Instead, architecture was meant to show the vibrant balance of yin and yang and to show the architects' and astronomers' special knowledge of placing and designing buildings. So before

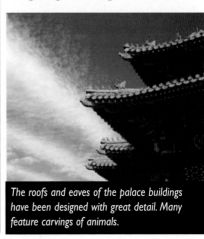

The roofs and eaves of the palace buildings have been designed with great detail. Many feature carvings of animals.

all the splendors of decoration and ornamentation were added, the City's architects had to plan where to put every building for the strongest benefit.

The Forbidden City faces south. It was laid out as a rectangle from north to south with its two main gates on the north and south walls and the buildings laid out as a grid inside. Each building within the walls was positioned according to its function and status. All buildings were constructed on painted wooden platforms to protect them against dampness. Also, giant bronze cauldrons filled with water were placed outside each building in case of fire. Chinese building procedures were the opposite of those used in most other countries. Instead of using walls and columns to hold up the roof, the Chinese first made the roof and then

Because most of the buildings in the City were made of wood, huge bronze cauldrons filled with water were placed outside each of the main buildings, in case fire broke out.

Tales & Customs — Paper Windows

Paper was invented in China in the 2nd century B.C. The earliest paper was made from plants such as hemp, but about a century later, the Chinese made paper from rice, bamboo, and wood. Many windows of the Forbidden City were called screens. These screens were filled with rice paper instead of glass. In the winter, the paper kept out cold air, and in the summer, it was pierced to let a gentle breeze into the rooms. The window paper was often replaced. Paper windows were commonly used across China because they were more economical than glass.

positioned columns beneath it—usually one in each corner was enough to hold up a roof that was heavy with tiles. Walls were merely screens and not used for support. Roof tiles were thick and semicircular, unlike Western tiles, which are usually flat.

Color and Symbolism

Symbols, usually representing long life, health, wealth, and power, were used throughout the Forbidden City. Colors are particularly significant. For instance, red means joy and yellow means glory. Both indicate imperial power. The main colors of the city were the crimson of the walls, representing joy, dignity, and solemnity; and the yellow glazed tiles, representing glory, Earth,

The colors on the roofs of each building in the Forbidden City traditionally represented the status or rank of the person who lived there.

life, and nourishment. Green represents harmony; white means purity and death; gray stands for disaster; and black stands for water. Platforms were white; pillars and walls were red. The roofs of all imperial buildings were yellow (the color reserved for the emperor), while temples had blue roofs. Purple often symbolizes joy, happiness, and heaven. Although the City was initially known as the "Purple Forbidden City," the color is not used extensively to paint the city. This early name is a reference to the palace of the Emperor of Heaven, which was believed to be the same color as the North-Star region in which it is believed to be located in the sky.

Animal statues guard many buildings in the Forbidden City. The male lion always has his right paw over a pomegranate, which was a symbol of power. Bronze turtles symbolize peace, and they also represent the emperor himself.

The rich use of color on all buildings in the Forbidden City usually has a purpose or symbolic meaning. For instance, on this building, red symbolizes happiness and yellow (or gold) stands for glory.

CHAPTER 2

The Forbidden City through History

During its time as a royal residence, fourteen emperors of the Ming dynasty and ten emperors of the Qing dynasty reigned in the Forbidden City. Although it was built for privilege and power, it became both a palace and a prison for those who lived there. Both the Ming and the Qing rulers believed that their dynasties would last forever, but five centuries after it was built, the last emperor left the Forbidden City only to come back and work on its grounds as a gardener.

How the City Was Founded

In 1211, the fierce and mighty warrior Genghis Khan took over China and set up the Mongol dynasty. Genghis Khan's grandson, Kublai Khan, later set up a new Mongol dynasty called the Yuan dynasty and built the first Forbidden City, which he called Danei, in Beijing in the 13th century. Mongol emperors ruled China for over a century until, in the mid-14th century, there was a series of floods, poor harvests, and famines. By 1325, one of the famines had killed nearly eight million people. The peasants believed that the Mongols

The grandson of Genghis Khan, Kublai Khan established the Yuan dynasty, which ruled until he was driven out by a rebellion by the people.

should have governed the country better and made sure that there was enough food for all. This caused several peasant revolts to break out across China in the 1350s. A peasant

named Zhu Yuanzhang then organized an army and conquered several regions across China. In 1368, he arrived in Beijing, expecting to face a Mongol army, but the Mongols had heard about him already and fled. So, he started a new dynasty, which he called Ming, ordered the destruction of the Mongol Yuan dynasty's Forbidden City, and settled with his new court in Nanjing, in the south. Calling himself Emperor Hongwu, Zhu Yuanzhang reigned until 1398, when his son Jianwen became the second Ming emperor. In 1402, Jianwen's uncle, Zhu Di, took the throne from Jianwen,

Time Line

1279	The Mongols conquer China.
1368	The Ming dynasty is founded by Chu Yuanchang, under whose leadership China regains independence from the Mongols.
1368	The renovation of the Great Wall of China begins.
1405	The pirate Zheng He Cheng Ho sails west with a fleet of three hundred ships, invading Sumatra and Ceylon and reaching the coast of Africa.
1421	Construction of the Forbidden City begins in Beijing.
1500	One hundred million people live under the Ming Empire.
1550	The renovation of the Great Wall is completed.

becoming the third emperor of the Ming dynasty and naming himself Yongle.

Chinese Control

Because the Ming emperors were Chinese, they felt more entitlement to reign over their own country and a Chinese military was established to defend their land against outsiders. Ming emperors reigned for 276 years, including 224 in the Forbidden City. Hongwu was a great leader and one of only three peasants ever to become an emperor in China. He kept the land tax low and the granaries stocked to guard against famine. However, he believed that agriculture should be the country's only source of

This 15th-century silk painting features two members of court during the Ming dynasty.

wealth and that trading with other countries was dishonorable. Hongwu admired military prowess, and he developed a strong military to defend against any enemies. He also took control of nearly all aspects of government so that no other group could gain enough power to overthrow him. Later, in the fourth year of his reign, Yongle decided to move his court back to the safer position of Beijing, and he had the Forbidden City rebuilt to keep himself and his court protected from enemies. He moved the position of his new Forbidden City slightly to the south of the former Mongol capital, so it would be in the exact center of Beijing, and spent a huge amount of money on rebuilding it. Once it was built, no other country in the world had a palace of such size, complexity, and grandeur, but then, no other country was as big. About 120 million people—

1557   Portugal establishes a trading post in Macao (first European settlement in the Far East).

1616   Nurhachi unifies the Manchus and creates the state of Qing (Jin) in northeastern China.

1637   The Manchus, led by Nurhachi's son Abahai, invade Korea, and Korea becomes a vassal state of the Manchus.

This vase painting shows gardeners watering tea plants. Tea was not a source of trade for China until the 17th century.

The Forbidden City

This silk painting from 1500 shows a priest standing in front of the Forbidden City.

more than the entire population of Europe—lived in China, and the emperor ruled over them all.

For more than 500 years, the emperors of two dynasties lived in luxury and seclusion, carrying out the affairs of state from the Forbidden City. Over that time, Yongle's original planning and ideas were hardly altered. The palace reflected power, wealth, and superiority. The Ming also poured money and manpower into rebuilding and extending the Great Wall of China, which was another way that the emperors protected themselves from outside attackers. Although

this autocratic way of life may have seemed like a good idea at the time, it had many flaws. Most people living in the Forbidden City, particularly the emperors and empresses themselves, became out of touch with the rest of China. They followed elaborate daily rituals that had little to do with the outside world. Inefficiency and corruption followed, and the ordinary people who lived in poverty outside the City often rose up and rebelled. Some emperors gave their servants or wives great responsibility, which meant that many people used their positions of power for personal advantage and not for the good of the people. A small number of people held too much power, although, at the time, it seemed to the Chinese that this was the only way to live.

Money, Books, and Art

From the beginning of the Ming dynasty, money was a problem. Paper notes and coins were considered to represent only

money that was kept in a country's treasury, usually in gold bars. When a country made more notes or coins than it had in gold, people began to lose faith in the money and it became devalued. At the beginning of the Ming dynasty, paper money (which the Chinese invented in the 10th century) was used. But Hongwu printed more paper money than he had gold in his treasury. By 1425, twenty-seven years after his death and five

One of the Seven Wonders of the World, the Great Wall of China was built more than 2,000 years ago to act as a defense against attackers. It stretches 4,163 miles (6,700 kilometers) from east to west.

years after the Forbidden City was built, Chinese currency was worth one-seventieth of its original value. So, paper money was abandoned and copper coins were used once more. However, the government did not make enough of these, and people began counterfeiting, which caused the coins to be worth even less. Despite this, there were great intellectual innovations in China under the Ming. One development of the dynasty was the fictional novel. Because they developed from Chinese storytellers, these books were written in everyday words, not in the exclusive language of the nobility, which most Chinese people could not understand. Chapters ended at the points where storytellers would have stopped to collect money from listeners, which is why they are gripping—listeners would have to pay to find out what happened next. Encyclopedias and dictionaries also began to be written during this time. This meant that many ordinary people could learn more. In 1615, a dictionary that reduced the number of "radicals" (the signs that are combined to make up Chinese characters) from over

1728	France establishes a trading post in Guangzhou (Canton).
1729	The emperor issues a decree banning the sale of opium.
1801	China's population reaches 295 million.
1830	Corruption, decentralization of power, popular rebellions.
1839	A Chinese attempt at suppressing the illicit British trade in opium causes the first Opium War.

Hand-dyeing silk was one of the specialized crafts that flourished under the Ming dynasty.

The Forbidden City

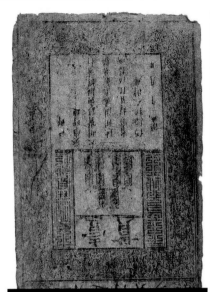

This banknote from the Ming dynasty was worth one thousand coins in 1374. Later, the value of currency dropped dramatically.

prints depicting interesting and amusing stories, while other craftspeople created the delicately patterned blue-and-white porcelain vases and jars in the Ming style that is so valuable now. Some Ming porcelain was decorated in three colors, but the best-known pieces are just blue and white. Although trade and merchants were looked down on, by the mid-15th century, China had established sea routes that were used for trade with Japan and south Asia, and it was far ahead of the rest of the world in naval capabilities. During the Ming dynasty, naval expeditions were extended, and some Europeans were permitted at court.

540 to 214 had a huge influence, because it made it much easier for people to read and write. Education was valued highly and educated Chinese people became interested in philosophy, religion, and art.

Two crafts that were invented by the Chinese in earlier times—wood-block printing and porcelain production—also became more popular during the Ming dynasty. Some craftspeople produced colorful wood-block

Downfall of the Ming Dynasty

Emperor Yongle aimed to restore

The novel was developed during the Ming dynasty. The illustration on this Ming vase shows some women reading a novel.

China to the dominant position it had held in Asia at the beginning of the 14th century. He established the Forbidden City to represent the almighty power of the Ming dynasty and believed that this would be the best way to rule China. But it had many faults, and the dynasty did not last. Although its power was great, it eventually fell. Most people who lived within the city walls were distant from their subjects, both mentally and physically, and did not know what their subjects really needed. Some emperors came to power as children and were overshadowed by their own employees, who took a lot of the control from them. For example, Emperor Wanli (1573–1620), tired of the burdens of power, gave most of his responsibilities to his courtiers. In addition, to support the extravagant lifestyle of the court, taxes were raised, angering ordinary people outside the Forbidden City. As with other dynasties, rebellion broke out outside the Forbidden City as people grew discontented. Meanwhile, the Manchu became angry that some cities in their own country, Manchuria, which was to the northeast of China, were being populated entirely by Chinese people. The Manchu began attacking these cities and forcing the Chinese out, eventually gaining control of the whole of Manchuria. They decided not to let it stop there and marched on to China. In 1644, a rebel named Li Zicheng gathered an army, entered Beijing, and seized power. On learning that Li Zicheng had seized Beijing, Emperor Chongzhen hanged himself in a park behind the Forbidden City. He was the last Ming emperor.

The Qing Dynasty

The first Qing emperor, named Shunzhi, was Manchurian. He started the dynasty by exterminating all the other rebels except for those from Manchuria. So, emperors of the Qing (pronounced *ching*) dynasty were foreign like the Yuan dynasty, making them the second foreign dynasty to rule China. The Qing ruled for 268 years, from 1644 to 1911, and the reigns of three of the first emperors of this dynasty were peaceful and prosperous. These three rulers provided strong leadership for 133 years. They were Kangxi (reigned 1662–1722), Yongzheng (reigned 1722–1736), and Qianlong (reigned 1736–1796). They retained many of the attitudes, ideas, and rules of the Ming and encouraged Chinese officials to serve them.

These distinctive blue-and-white patterns are a feature of the main Ming porcelain style.

1900	The anti-Western Boxer (Yihetuan) rebellion is crushed by foreign troops (Russia, Britain, France, Japan, United States), and Tsu Hsi flees to the mountains. China's population is 467 million.
1911	Riots cause the collapse of the Qing dynasty, and the Republic of China is born, but power is seized by Yuan Shikai and 11 million die.

The Forbidden City

Despite the fact that the Manchu were renowned for their military power, the Qing dynasty was a relatively peaceful period.

They continued to modernize farming, which the Ming had started, and they organized their government in an extremely efficient way. During the period, taxes were generally light and international trade grew. Books, printing, painting, and porcelain production improved even more, leading to a revival of arts and learning. But Qing emperors and courts were set in their ways and did not change much in the following centuries. When the West wanted to trade with them for valuable Chinese goods, Qing emperors feared that wealthy European merchants would undermine their authority. The Qing restricted trade heavily, and so prevented the Chinese economy from growing as fast as it could have. Later, wars with Western powers—including Britain and France—and Japan, left them weakened. Eventually, internal rebellions left the Qing unable to cope with the needs of such a vast country. Beyond the walls of the City, over the centuries, great cultural, social and political, and technological changes had occurred. But within the walls, life remained inflexible and disciplined. Then, one day, the outside world caught up with it.

No Longer Forbidden

As a result of war, certain Chinese cities were taken over by some more powerful Western countries. China was being weakened, but inside the Forbidden City, no one knew. Eventually, on October 10, 1911,

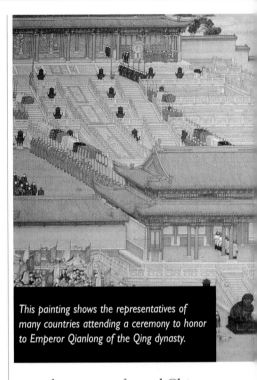

This painting shows the representatives of many countries attending a ceremony to honor to Emperor Qianlong of the Qing dynasty.

a revolution transformed China from an empire into a republic, and outside the Forbidden City, the Nationalist Party took control. In 1912, the last Qing emperor, Puyi, abdicated because the Prime Minister had taken control of China, declaring it a new republic. Puyi kept the title of emperor, and the royal family was allowed to stay in the Forbidden City. While there, he was taught English until 1924, when he was forced to sign

Time Line

1924	Puyi, the last emperor, leaves the Forbidden City.	
1931	Japan invades Manchuria. Great floods occur in China.	
1934	In order to avoid persecution by the Nationalist government, Mao Zedong leads the Long March of the communist Red Army (170,000 die).	
1937	Japan invades China and captures Nanking.	
1945	World War II ends, and Japan is forced to retreat (20 million Chinese dead).	
1945	At the end of World War II, the Korean Peninsula is occupied by the Soviet Union (north) and the United States (south).	
1948	Communist North Korea declares independence.	
1949	Mao Zedong proclaims the People's Republic of China.	

marshes and deserts, led by Mao Zedong, a former teacher. Only one out of every five people who set out on the march survived. They made Yan'an their headquarters until 1946, when fighting between the Nationalist Party and the Communist Party turned into civil war. After nearly three years of war, the Communists won, and Mao Zedong stood at the Gate of Heavenly Peace, in front of the Forbidden City, to announce the founding of the People's Republic of China. The new Communist government said it would create a new, fair society for all, completely different from the one that had allowed one man to have total power. Mao Zedong's policies tried to destroy traditional customs, books, and clothes. But under the new government, people who spoke out against Communism were either killed or sent to work in

labor camps. Thousands of people were exiled, and any trade with the West was stopped. In getting rid of the emperors, China had simply replaced them with another strict regime. The ten years before Chairman Mao's death in 1976 were nicknamed the "Ten Years of Chaos."

documents saying that he was just an ordinary Chinese citizen and made to leave the Forbidden City. After 1927, the Communist Party broke with the Nationalists. By the end of 1934, the "Red Army" (about 100,000 people who believed in Communism), left Jiangxi to travel to Yan'an. They marched through many provinces, climbed over eighteen mountain ranges, crossed twenty-four rivers, and trekked through

The last emperor to reside in the Forbidden City was the Qing emperor, Puyi. In 1912, Puyi abdicated the throne, and China became a republic.

1950	Communist North Korea, helped by China, attacks noncommunist South Korea, but the invasion fails after the United States intervenes.
1950	Mao orders the persecution of landlords, causing the deaths of about one million people.
1958	Mao's "Great Leap Forward" causes a famine that leads to the deaths of between 16 and 30 million people.

1966	Mao launches the "Cultural Revolution." Millions die over the next three years.
1972	United States president Richard Nixon formally recognizes Communist China as a country.
1981	The Chinese Communist Party formally condemns Mao for the economic disasters his policies brought about from 1957 until his death in 1976.

CHAPTER 3 · *Exploring the Forbidden City*

The Forbidden City is deep in the center of Beijing. It is divided into three main areas. The first part, at the south end, is the great courtyard that lies between the Meridian Gate and the Gate of Supreme Harmony. This was where people waited if they wanted to see the emperor. The second area is the Outer Court, which contains three palaces in which both business and ceremonies were carried out. Located at the northern end of the city, the third area is the Inner Court—the tightly guarded and private living quarters of the emperor and his family.

Pages 20–21: The Entrance

 Gate of Heavenly Peace

 Meridian Gate

 Golden River

 Gate of Supreme Harmony

Pages 22–23: The Outer Court

 Hall of Supreme Harmony

 Outer Court

 Hall of Central Harmony

 Hall of Preserving Harmony

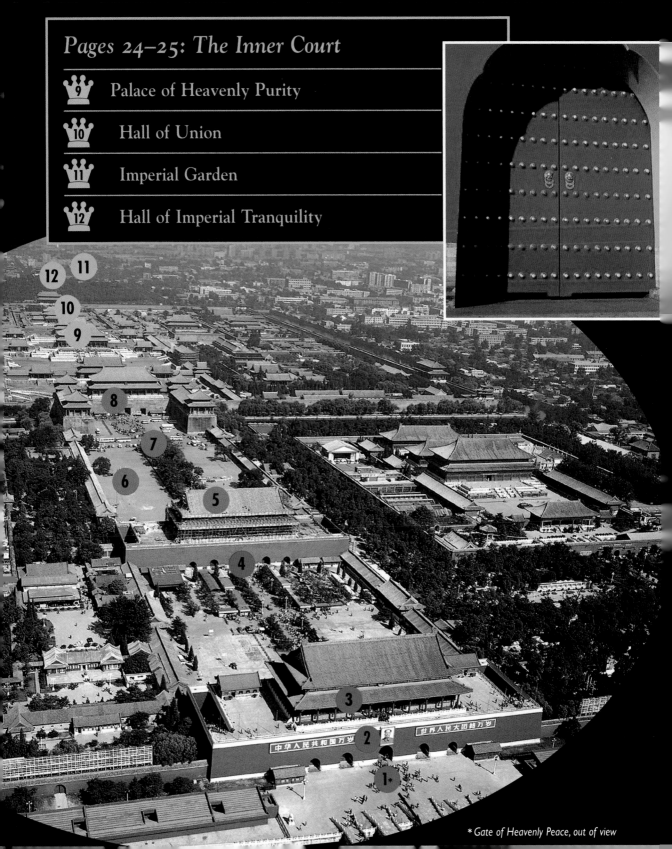

*Gate of Heavenly Peace, out of view

Gate of Heavenly Peace, out of view

 Gate of Heavenly Peace

Originally, there were eight gates that had to be passed through before reaching the Great Courtyard. Not all of the gates are still there, but one gate in particular leads up to the beginning of the Great Courtyard. This is the Gate of Heavenly Peace, or Tiananmen. Tiananmen Gate was originally built during the Ming dynasty, and it was rebuilt in 1651. It marks the passage from the Imperial City to the Forbidden City. There are balconies over the gate, from which the emperor would announce important messages or send off his generals with great ceremony if they were going to war. Even now, the Chinese army raises the Chinese flag from this site every day at dawn. The square to the south of Tiananmen was the site of the most shocking event in recent Chinese history—the massacre by the government of over 2,000 prodemocracy protesters in June 1989.

The tallest building of the Forbidden City is its main entrance. The imposing Meridian Gate is 262 feet (80 m) tall. The emperor used to survey his troops from the great pavilion above the central gate.

 Meridian Gate

The Meridian Gate stands at the southern entrance of the Forbidden City. This gate, which was built in 1417, stands imposingly in the massive outer wall and leads directly into the Great Courtyard. At 131 feet (40 m) long, the Meridian Gate is the tallest building in the Forbidden City. Chinese emperors believed that the gateway lay on a significant line in the center of the world and directly beneath the Sun. The grand gate has five openings and is topped by five pavilions named Five Phoenix Tower. There were strict rules to follow when people entered the Forbidden City. The only person other than the emperor who was allowed through the central gateway was the empress on her wedding day.

 ## Golden River

The moat around the Forbidden City was called the Outer Golden Water River, or the Golden River. The Meridian Gate opens onto a courtyard that is 656 feet (200 m) long and 426 feet (130 m) wide. Here, the Golden River continues to flow but as a smaller river, which, when inside the City, is called the Inner Golden Water River. Five gleaming, white marble bridges span the Inner Golden Water River. The bridges were decorated with marble balustrades carved with dragons and a phoenix. Water from the river was close by in case of fire.

The Golden River flows in an arc shape and can be crossed by any one of five marble bridges.

The double-roofed Gate of Supreme Harmony stands on a terrace in front of a large marble square.

Gate of Supreme Harmony

On the other side of this courtyard is the Gate of Supreme Harmony. This gate rises up across the Inner Golden Water, blocking off the next and largest courtyard, the Outer Court. The Gate of Supreme Harmony is the tallest gatehouse in the Forbidden City. Two large bronze lions guard the stairs to the gatehouse. These are classic Chinese symbols of power and dignity—guardians of the rich and the powerful. The lion on the right is the male, and he has a ball under his foot, symbolizing that imperial power extended worldwide. The lioness, to the left, puts her front left paw on a lion cub, symbolizing a prosperous, growing family.

The Forbidden City

 ## Hall of Supreme Harmony

Through the Gate of Supreme Harmony is the Outer Court, which contains three Halls of Harmony. The first, the Hall of Supreme Harmony, is the largest hall in the Forbidden City. This is the most important building in the City, first built in about 1418 and restored in the 17th century. Great ceremonies, banquets, coronations, and meetings were held here. The large bronze turtle at the entrance has a removable lid. On special occasions, incense was burned in it so that smoke billowed from the mouth. Inside, the hall is decorated in red and gold, with twenty-four marble columns beneath a double-curved roof and a richly decorated dragon throne. Around the throne are two bronze cranes, an elephant-shaped incense burner, and tripods in the shape of mythical beasts.

The grand throne platform resides inside the Hall of Supreme Harmony in the Outer Court of the Forbidden City.

Outer Court

The massive Outer Court is about 323,000 square feet (30,000 square meters) in area, and its three halls are vast and imposing palaces, built for important functions in the daily life of the emperor. There are no trees on the square as the emperors were believed to be Sons of Heaven, and, therefore, occupy the highest position in the country. An "imperial road" crosses the court. This is a pathway marked in stone across the brick-paved courtyard. At ceremonies, guards would be stationed on the great terrace of the Outer Court, carrying between them more than two hundred ceremonial objects of silver and gold, and two orchestras would play. Scents would rise from bronze urns that were filled with either burning pine branches or scented oil floating on water.

The Outer Court was the open space within the City in which much of the public imperial business and festivities took place.

♛ Hall of Central Harmony

Next in the Outer Court, running in a line, is the Hall of Central Harmony, which is square in shape—unlike the other halls of the Outer Court, which are rectangular—with a curved pyramid shaped roof. This is the smallest of the three main halls in the Outer Court. It is where the emperor prepared himself before entering the Hall of Supreme Harmony.

The smallest building of the three in the Outer Court, the Hall of Central Harmony was where the emperor spent a few private moments before facing his assembly.

♛ Hall of Preserving Harmony

The third hall in the Outer Court is the Hall of Preserving Harmony, which has the same design as the Hall of Supreme Harmony but is smaller. Apart from the empress on her wedding day, no women were admitted to any of the three halls in the Outer Court. Three doorways on the north side of the Hall of Preserving Harmony open onto steps, and a great carved marble ramp leads to the Gate of Heavenly Purity, which separated the official Outer Court from the private Inner Court.

The massive red columns that support the exterior of the Hall of Preserving Harmony mirror those of the Hall's interior.

The Forbidden City

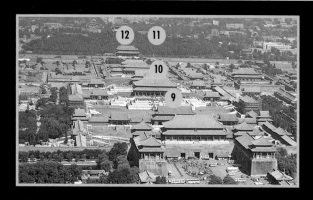

 9 Palace of Heavenly Purity

The Inner Court was the most private of all parts of the Forbidden City. It was where the emperor and his family lived. The first and most important building in this court is the Palace of Heavenly Purity, which housed the throne room and the imperial bedchamber. It was also used as offices by later emperors. Banquets were held in the Inner Court for New Year's and other festivals, and emperors' coffins waited in this court before their funerals. The throne is magnificent—gold, decorated with glittering rubies and emeralds. Behind the throne is a gilded screen covered with quotations from ancient Chinese philosophers written in beautiful calligraphy.

10 Hall of Union

The second of the Inner Court palaces is built on a square, like the Hall of Central Harmony, and is called the Hall of Union. With its water clock and a golden ceiling with a golden ball suspended from the center, this was the empresses' throne room. Leading on from the Hall of Union, is the Palace of Earthly Tranquility, in which Ming empresses lived. It was also used as a special wedding chamber and a shrine where some emperors worshiped.

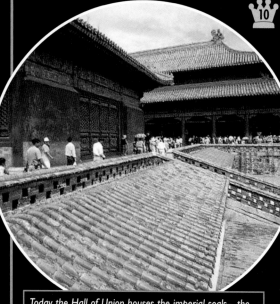

Today the Hall of Union houses the imperial seals—the emperors' signature stamps. Each stamp is made of gold, jade, and sandalwood.

The Palace of Heavenly Purity is one of the original Ming buildings built in 1420 for the emperor to live in.

 Imperial Garden

To the north, through the Gate of Earthly Tranquility, is the Imperial Garden, which spreads over about 129,200 square feet (12,000 sq m). It was designed to be a space for relaxation and contemplation. This is where emperors came to rest. Garden planning in China was an extension of architectural planning and design. The

The rocks and carefully cultivated plants in the Imperial Garden were designed to inspire peace.

landscaped gardens contained purposefully placed rocks, trees, rock gardens, walkways, and pavilions. Emperor Qianlong wrote of the garden, "Every ruler, when he has returned from audience and has finished his public duties, must have a garden in which he may stroll, look around and relax his heart."

Hall of Imperial Tranquility

In the center of the garden is the Hall of Imperial Tranquility (or Peace), the best preserved of all the Ming buildings. Inside is a statue of Xuan Wu, the water god, who required lots of encouragement in the form of daily offerings to protect the whole of the Forbidden City from fire. Nearby, there are many other buildings surrounding the three courts, including living quarters for the emperor's family and servants, libraries, theaters, kitchens, and storage halls. One distinctive building within view is the Temple of Heaven, a circular building situated on a three-layered platform.

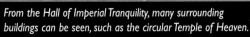

From the Hall of Imperial Tranquility, many surrounding buildings can be seen, such as the circular Temple of Heaven.

At the end of the 18th century, about 9,000 people lived in the Forbidden City. Chinese people believed that the emperor was the "Son of Heaven" and the link between the people and God. No one questioned how emperors lived—they had complete power and could do as they pleased. This power protected emperors but also isolated them. Although many emperors improved life for their subjects, most had no idea about the hardships many people outside the Forbidden City suffered.

The Emperors

Under the Ming emperors, the population of China doubled. Educated Chinese people learned about philosophy, religion, and art. Yongle and emperors after him expanded sea trade and

Under the Ming dynasty, educated people became learned and mastered the arts. This Ming silk painting depicts a household scene.

expeditions, as well as industry. They also encouraged eminent Europeans to enter the Forbidden City and meet with important Chinese officials. But for all this forward thinking, the Ming dynasty became weak when its emperors became too isolated and unaware of the poverty of some of their subjects or gave too much power to their immediate servants. When the Qing dynasty came to power, its leaders had other ideas. They tried a new method of government, giving power to officials other than only those in the Inner Court. Emperor Kangxi, the longest ruling emperor, secured the borders of China, improved agriculture, built-up the textile industry, and also encouraged arts, crafts, and book publishing. Some of this helped peasants all over China, giving them valuable work. Kangxi's successors, Yongzheng, his eleventh son, and

Qianlong, his grandson, continued to strengthen the country. All emperors spent most of their days attending to official duties. The daily running of the palace was ruled by codes of behavior (protocol) and rituals. To relax, emperors walked in the Imperial Garden; prayed or meditated; played chess; wrote poetry and calligraphy; or played the qin, a seven-stringed instrument. Some also raised grasshoppers.

Eating was a big part of an emperor's day. Unless they were at a banquet, emperors ate alone. They were served breakfast at dawn, lunch at midday, and dinner at sunset. Generally there were eight main dishes, four side dishes, two or three hot soups, firepots, steamed buns, rice,

Emperor Qianlong (1711–1799) was the fourth emperor of the Qing dynasty.

cakes, and herbal teas. Any food that was left over was sent to their wives and concubines. Any remaining food after that was given to the servants. Court life was organized around tradition and formal procedures. Courtiers had to follow set codes of dress and behavior. Ministers and officials had to prostrate themselves nine times when they appeared before the emperor, which meant bowing, kneeling, and touching the ground with their foreheads nine times.

Qianlong

Qianlong was sophisticated and learned. He admired and enjoyed all the arts and regularly visited the palace workshops to see artifacts being made. Beginning at the age of six, he worked hard

Tales & Customs — Special Events

A number of special events took place at the Meridian Gate (the southern entrance to the Forbidden City). On the equivalent of October 1, the emperor would make public the solar calendar for the coming year. This calendar indicated the days on which the various annual ceremonies would be held. In ancient times, emperors gave food to ministers at the Gate to mark important days in the year. Also, after a war, emperors would receive captives at the Meridian Gate.

The Forbidden City

The art of calligraphy flourished under Qianlong's leadership.

every day at calligraphy, writing poetry, painting, and reading the classics and works of philosophy. He had several advisors around him in the Forbidden Palace, such as an Italian priest who was also a painter and architect and a French mathematician and astronomer. He commissioned many books and works of art and collected many ornaments and artworks, including paintings, carved jade, and works of calligraphy, and he kept a detailed catalog of everything. During his reign, the arts—such as painting, calligraphy, and enamel and inlay work—really flourished. Qianlong's workdays usually began at about 3 A.M. and continued until about 10 P.M. From within the city, he discussed problems of the country with his ministers, planned solutions, and initiated military expeditions. However,

Tales & Customs — Clever Beasts

In one of the great halls of the Forbidden City, the Hall of Central Harmony, there are two golden unicorns, one on each side of the throne. These were called "luduan" in Chinese and were believed to be capable of traveling about 5,590 miles (9,000 km) in one day and speaking many languages. Since these divine beasts could see and tell so much, they were put beside the throne to indicate the wisdom and foresight of the emperors. Also, on either side of the throne are sedan chairs that were used to transport emperors around the Forbidden City.

his reign was not perfect, and he gave too much power to some of his favorite people. Power made many favorites greedy, but if the favoritism ended, the penalty was often severe. For instance, Qianlong gave a huge amount of power to a Manchu general named Heshen. Heshen spent a lot of money and was believed to have too much influence over Qianlong. So, when Qianlong died, Heshen was ordered to commit suicide. Emperors had several wives and additional female companions. (Emperors were allowed to have these female companions, who were like unofficial wives and were known as concubines.) For example, Qianlong had two official wives and twenty-nine concubines (and twenty-six children). Qianlong was also a great military man. A tolerant ruler, he allowed several religions to be practiced during his reign, including Taoism (although he limited the Taoists' power), Christianity, Confucianism, and Islam, in spite of the fact that China's primary religion was Buddhism. After sixty years of rule, he retired out of respect for his grandfather, Kangxi, who had reigned for sixty-one years.

The Succession

Deciding who would be the next emperor was a problem because emperors usually had several sons by different wives and concubines. A system developed in which the emperor's choice of successor was kept secret until after his death. The emperor would write the name of his choice on a document and keep it concealed within his robes.

These ceramic figurines from the Qianlong period depict female attendants bearing food.

The emperor Qianlong formally receives a party of visitors at the Forbidden City.

He also would have written the same name on another document and put it into a sealed box. Upon the emperor's death, both documents would be taken and compared. One name would be on both documents, and that person was the new emperor.

The Last Emperor

The last emperor, Puyi, took the throne in 1908, at the age of three. He was forced to abdicate in 1912 but stayed in the Forbidden City until 1924, learning to read and write and practicing calligraphy for hours every day. During this time, he also learned to ride a bicycle and play tennis. He remained a symbol of importance for many people.

Women of the Court

Twelve palaces—six on each side of the Inner Court—were homes for the wives, concubines, and other female relatives of the

Women of the court were governed by strict protocols. The ivory sculpture above depicts Kuan Yin, a goddess from the Qian period. She was believed to possess all the ideal womanly virtues, such as compassion, mercy, and modesty.

emperor. Behind these two groups of palaces were the green-roofed buildings reserved for the infant princes. The only woman who did not live in these palaces was the emperor's mother—the highest ranking woman in the country, who was known as the dowager empress. The dowager empress lived in the Palace of Benevolent Tranquility, a large complex of palaces to the east of the Gate of Heavenly Purity.

Empresses, other wives, and concubines were always of high birth before they entered the Forbidden City. Once married to the emperor, each of his wives received an important rank, although the emperor always had a "number one wife"—the empress—who was the second most important woman in the city. Although the dowager

Tales & Customs — Every Detail Counts

No detail was spared in ensuring that the Forbidden City was perfectly built. Even the ground of the courtyard was laid in a particular way—seven layers of bricks lengthwise and eight layers of bricks across, each on top of the other, totaling fifteen layers. The purpose of this layering was to protect the City against assassins who might dig tunnels into the palace. The bricks were specially made to sound nice when walked upon. The rooms on each side of the courtyard were said to serve as warehouses for storing valuables such as furs, porcelain, silver, tea, silk, and satin.

Emperors were entitled to have more than one wife at a time. This 19th-century painting shows a wedding ceremony taking place during the Qing Dynasty.

empress was more important, the empress was the person who governed the affairs of the Inner Court. Depending on their positions, wives had to follow rules, such as rules about the number of pearls on their hats, the color and quality of their ceremonial clothes, or the amount and type of food they were served. Different ranking wives ate from different colored crockery. Only the emperor and empress were entitled to use real gold, or "radiant yellow" porcelain. All Qing wives and concubines were Manchu—no Chinese women were permitted. Imperial women made silk, prepared cakes, and looked after the children. Upon the death of the emperor, wives and concubines retired to a vast complex of palaces to the west of the Inner Court. Ming women had their feet bound as children so that they grew up with small feet, a feature that was seen as the height of attractiveness in the Ming era. Qing women were forbidden to do this because foot-binding was considered too "Ming" for them. Instead, they wore shoes with extremely high porcelain platform soles.

Dragon Lady

In 1861, when her husband, Emperor Xianfeng, died at the age of thirty, Empress Cixi refused to retire to one of the outer palaces, as tradition demanded. Instead, she ruled as regent for her son—Xianfeng's only son—who was five years old and only lived until his teens.

The Dowager Empress Cixi (1835–1908) ruled as regent for her son after her husband died.

When he died, she placed her four-year-old nephew on the throne. He only lived until his mid-twenties. In effect, Empress Cixi ruled China for forty-eight years, sitting on her throne each morning to receive visitors and eventually dying in 1908, when two-year-old Puyi came to the throne. Empress Cixi rebuilt many of the palaces in the Forbidden City, restoring, repairing, and improving many of the original buildings that had been built by Yongle. In 1885, in the year of her fiftieth birthday, she had the Palace of Concentrated Beauty completely refurbished. She had a little theater built in one area of the palace, and in the courtyard,

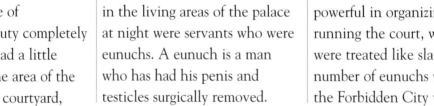

Many eunuchs resided in the Forbidden City. This photograph of a eunuch of the last dynasty was taken by Henri Cartier Bresson in 1949.

bronze dragons and deer—good luck symbols—were added. Cixi, along with 180 servants, lived in this palace for ten years, before moving on to the Palace of Peaceful Longevity.

Dowager Empress Cixi is called "the Dragon Lady" because of her ruthlessness, drive, and cunning.

Other People in the Forbidden City

While women and children in the emperor's family lived in the palace, adult males generally did not. The only men allowed in the living areas of the palace at night were servants who were eunuchs. A eunuch is a man who has had his penis and testicles surgically removed.

Usually taking place before puberty, the operation prevents the male body from producing testosterone so that a eunuch never develops certain male characteristics, such as facial hair and a deep voice, and cannot produce children. Eunuchs were considered safe and loyal members of the royal court. Some eunuchs became extremely powerful in organizing and running the court, while others were treated like slaves. The number of eunuchs working in the Forbidden City varied greatly

Tales & Customs — Unusual Eunuchs

Ordinary Chinese men were not allowed inside the Forbidden City. All male workers in the City were eunuchs. Eunuchs tested everything on behalf of the emperor. They even tasted his food and tested his urine to make sure he was healthy. Young princes were raised almost exclusively by eunuchs. There are several stories of corrupt and power-hungry eunuchs who were believed to have manipulated the attitudes and character of the young princes in their care to suit their own needs.

This painting features court ladies combing and spinning silk during the Northern Song dynasty in the early 12th century. Silk weaving was one of many artistic enterprises prized at court.

and artistic skills. In addition, priestess-magicians performed rituals in the city. With accompaniment from drummers, they went into a trances in which they made predictions and performed exorcisms. Priests of other religions—in particular, Buddhism—were always present.

according to the dynasty. In the Ming court, it is said that there were about 20,000, but Kangxi reduced the number to 9,000 and Qianlong to 3,000. At the fall of the Qing dynasty, there were no more than 1,500. One might wonder why anyone would become a eunuch, but for most of them, it was their only hope of escaping poverty, and they either volunteered or were sold by their parents. Sadly, only half of them survived the operation that made them eunuchs. Maids also worked in the Forbidden City. They entered at the age of thirteen and spent a year training in a particular skill. Then, they worked for about three or four years and were sent out of the city to get married. Maids who left the Forbidden City were never allowed to return.

Some people were employed in the Forbidden City who lived outside. These people included guards who protected the city, domestic servants who carried out the lowliest tasks, and gardeners. Some scholars entered the Forbidden City to take exams. Those allowed in were chosen by an entrance exam, which was very difficult. Those who passed were given another exam in the Forbidden City that was even tougher, creating a tradition of pride in academic achievement.

Throughout the history of the city, various people of different religions and races often passed through. For example, Jesuit missionaries from Europe spent time there. They were respected for their scientific knowledge

People of many different religions, such as European Jesuit missionaries like the one pictured above, were drawn to China.

Many festivals were celebrated in the Forbidden City. The most important of these was the New Year's celebration. The old Chinese calendar was different from the calendar used in the West, with its months following the Moon rather than the Sun. Because of this, every few years an extra month had to be added to it. Dates of events vary from year to year; the Chinese New Year falls between the middle of January and early March.

Chinese New Year

Traditionally, the Chinese New Year was a time to make a complete new start. All the rooms in the Forbidden City were cleaned. Everything, including pictures, statues, and furniture, was thoroughly scrubbed. The empress oversaw this, having first chosen a lucky day on which to start the cleaning, as everything followed good omens or lucky signs. Then special guests were invited to the celebrations. Everyone had new clothes for the last day of the old year, and even the royal elephants had new headwear. Special steamed—not baked—cakes were made to be placed before the Buddhas and other religious statues around the city. It was believed that the higher the cakes rose, the happier the gods became. In addition, small plates of dates and fresh fruit decorated with evergreen plants were placed before images of Buddha, and glass dishes filled with sweets were offered to the "god of the kitchen." This god was important because the

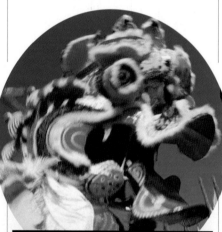

Colorful sights such as people in dragon costumes can be seen during Chinese New Year celebrations.

Chinese believed that on the twenty-third day of the last Moon, the god of the kitchen went to visit the King of Heaven, to whom he reported on all that everyone had been doing in the Forbidden City that year.

The sweets were meant to stick his mouth together to prevent him from telling too much.

Just before New Year's Eve, all the emperor's guests and high-ranking members of the court received beautifully written letters from the emperor, wishing them luck, long life, and prosperity. Gifts were exchanged, with the most lavish gifts given to the emperor and empress. Then, the emperor gave out small amounts of money to everyone, which were thought to bring good luck. Festivities followed, lasting all night.

Festival of Lanterns

The New Year's celebrations ended on the fifteenth day of the first moon with the Festival of Lanterns. Brightly colored gauze lanterns shaped like dragons, animals, flowers, and fruits were strung across the courtyards, and

Color features strongly in the Festival of Lanterns, during which people dress up in colorful costumes and lanterns adorn the streets.

everyone wore colorful costumes. There was music and dancing, and the evening ended with a grand fireworks display. The fireworks told stories about the history of China or lit up the sky as sparkling flowers and fruits. Portable wooden houses were made especially for the Imperial family and guests, from which they could watch while keeping out of the cold night air. But because wooden houses and fireworks don't always mix, huge cauldrons of water were placed nearby in case of fire.

Fireworks are generally a big part of celebrations and festivals in the Forbidden City.

Other Ceremonies

The Outer Court was the site of most other festivities, such as the accession of a new emperor to the throne, birthdays, weddings, and the arrival of spring or fall. These events were all announced by drum rolls and music. In the courtyard before the Hall of Supreme Harmony, rows of court officials took up positions according to rank, guided by bronze markers set in the ground.

Tales & Customs — Weddings and Parties

Emperors' weddings were extremely ornate. Most people dressed in red and gold, and the bride had her head covered throughout the ceremony. There was a lot of dancing and music at all festivals in the Forbidden City. Many dances told stories about the emperor's ancestors. Each year, near the Imperial Garden, in the courtyard of the Study of Fresh Fragrance, Emperor Qianlong had a two-story theater-banquet-and-concert hall built for the imperial family to celebrate the Spring Festival.

Many of the beautiful ornaments and furnishings were either taken from the Forbidden City or damaged. While many fires were accidental, some fires were started deliberately by eunuchs and court officials who could get rich on repair bills. Sadly, rare books, paintings, and examples of calligraphy were also lost. In the last years of the empire, Emperor Puyi stole or pawned many cultural relics. In the 20th century, there were two major lootings of the Forbidden City, and many of its valuable relics were taken away. Today, many of these items are in museums elsewhere.

Relics Recovered

In the 1950s, after more than ten years of hard work, searching, and questioning by Chinese government officials, about 710,000 relics from the Forbidden City during the Qing dynasty were retrieved, some of them the same objects that Puyi had pawned to make money for himself. At the same time, through donations and even more rigorous searching, over 220,000 further objects were found and added to the collection. These included ancient paintings, ornaments, scrolls, and examples of intricate calligraphy. To keep these safe, from the 1950s onward, the museum's storehouses were completely repaired to provide a moisture- and insect-proof

This vase was made during the Qianlong period of the Qing dynasty and is part of the museum collection today.

environment for the treasures. In the 1990s, an even newer storehouse with space for over 600,000 items—and with controls for maintaining constant temperature and humidity, as well as defenses against fire and theft—was built. A workshop that had been established in the 1950s was extended in the 1980s to include a scientific and technological restoration department. These additions not only carried forward the traditions of craftsmanship, but also drew upon the discoveries of the natural sciences to help with the restoration of damaged relics and artifacts. Gradually, the Forbidden City's valuables are being restored and repaired.

Today, the Forbidden City has more than ten museums, and the Wen Hua Hall stores more than 10 million official documents drawn up over 500 years by the central and local governments of the Ming and Qing dynasties. It is the largest and most valuable collection of historical records in China. The Imperial Library keeps the Si Ku Quan Shu, a 79,337-volume series of historical records collected over ten years by China's most accomplished scholars. These records tell about how the Forbidden City looked and how it was run each day.

Superstition

Because yellow was the symbol of the Chinese royal family, it was the dominant color of the Forbidden City. Most roofs were built with yellow tiles, many decorations in the palaces were painted yellow, and even bricks on the ground were made yellow by a special process. Still, a few palace buildings had black or green tiles instead of yellow. For instance, there were three palace buildings behind the palaces of the emperors' wives that were built with green tiles. These were the residences of the Qing princes. According to superstition, only green tiles could be used for the Qing high-ranking nobles, such as princes. Yellow—the color of the Sun — could not be used and was

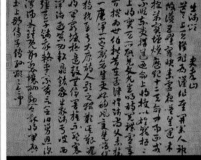
Written documents held at the museum, such as the "Ode to Dispatching Troops" above is of great historic and artistic value today.

only allowed for the emperor himself. On the other hand, the Wenyuan Pavilion, or the royal library, was built with black tiles. According to the ancient Chinese theory of the Five Elements, black represents water. Because the Wenyuan Pavilion was used for storing books, it was a fire risk. Therefore, in line with the superstitious idea of the ancients, black tiles—symbolizing water—were used to counteract this risk. Purple and red were also imperial colors, and these colors are used for many of the decorations inside the palaces.

Tourists can see a small-scale version of the Forbidden City at the Imperial Palace Museum.

Tales & Customs — The Five Elements

Some features of the city—such as the black tile roof of Wenyuan Pavilion—reflect the influence of the Chinese belief in the Five Elements:

1. *Wood burns producing fire;*
2. *Fire leaves behind Earth;*
3. *Earth is the source of metal;*
4. *Metal liquifies into flowing liquid like water;*
5. *Water then becomes the nourishment of the wood.*

The Forbidden City

The Nine-Dragon Screen

Animals and numbers were also symbolic to the people of China during the Ming and Qing dynasties. Behind the Hall of Preserved Harmony, in the middle of the stairway, is the Nine-Dragon Screen. This is the biggest stone sculpture in the Forbidden City. Anyone who was caught touching this holy stone would be punished by death. One of three such screens built in China, the Nine-Dragon Screen at the Forbidden City is the largest. Built in 1771, during the reign of Emperor Qianlong, it is 11.5 feet (3.5 m) high and about 98 feet (30 m) long. Made up of 270 tiles, it shows nine dragons playing with pearls against a background of the sea and clouds. The screen is colored in shades of yellow, blue, white, and violet. The number of dragons symbolizes the supreme importance of the emperor. Nine is the highest single-digit number, while five is in the middle, between one and nine. The screen has nine dragons with five additional dragons on the border. The Chinese dragon represented heaven and the power of man. It was also the emblem of the imperial family. So, the Nine-Dragon Screen represents the emperor as the Son of Heaven. The belly of the third white dragon has a piece of wood sticking out of it. It is said that the dragon broke when it was being made. Had his mistake been discovered, the craftsman making the dragon would have been punished with death. A carpenter repaired it with a piece of wood to keep the damage from being spotted by the emperor's inspector.

Man-made Hill

Overlooking the Forbidden City is a man-made hill created using the dirt taken from excavations of the imperial moat in 1420. According to ancient Chinese beliefs, this hill would protect the Forbidden City from any evil spirits swooping in from the north, which feng shui says bring only death and misery. Emperor Yongle ordered flowers and trees

The Nine-Dragon Wall is the biggest stone sculpture in the Forbidden City. As was the case with the animals in most Chinese sculptures, dragons were symbolic to the Chinese people. Among other things, dragons were the symbol of the royal family.

Tales & Customs — Fine Dining

Under the reign of Daoguang (1821–1850), the kitchens of the Forbidden City contained more than 3,000 gold and silver items. Some gold cups and bowls weighed over 300 pounds (140 kilograms). Silver plates weighed up to 2,756 pounds (1,250 kg). Meals were great occasions in the Forbidden City. Every day, Emperor Puyi might have ten different courses for breakfast, followed by up to twenty courses for lunch. Puyi's great aunt, the Dowager Empress Cixi, chose from up to 150 different dishes every day, and she ate with golden chopsticks.

to be planted on the hill and cranes and deer to be raised there. Every year, on the ninth day of the ninth month, he climbed up the hill and prayed for an uneventful year. The hill was called Coal Hill, and it is believed that a hidden coal supply was buried there for the imperial family. It was on Coal Hill that Congzhen, the last Ming emperor, hung himself.

Ming Tombs

About 31 miles (50 km) northwest of Beijing, the Ming emperors were buried in tombs. The Ming tombs cover an area of over 25 miles (40 km) in circumference, and thirteen of the sixteen emperors of the Ming dynasty (1368–1644) are buried there. At the gate to the tomb area stands a marble archway that leads to the Sacred, or Spirit, Way. Large stone animal statues line both sides of this area, including a statue of a giant tortoiselike animal. Excavations of the Ming tombs have, over the years, uncovered many rare treasures, such as the golden royal crowns and the silk robes that the emperors used to wear.

Looking south from Coal Hill in Jingshan Park provides a clear view of the Forbidden City.

This ceremonial robe would have been worn by Emperor Qianlong. It is currently on display at the museum.

For the five hundred years that the Ming and Qing emperors ruled, no one was allowed inside the Forbidden City except the emperor's family and officials. Since 1925, however, it has been a public museum. Since 1987, it has been a World Heritage site. Every day, crowds of people pass through the Meridian Gate, which used to be the emperor's entrance; the Gate of Spiritual Valor, in the north; and the two smaller gates to the east and west. Visitors view the magnificent architecture, furnishings, statues, and gardens, as well as the collection of over one million artifacts.

Visiting the City

Now open to everyone, the Forbidden City remains a symbol of Chinese rule and imperial power. It is a timeless example of ancient Chinese architecture and of the principles of feng shui. Certain buildings within the city take turns displaying art collections and housing temporary exhibitions. The most precious items are exhibited in the Palace of Peaceful Longevity. Every year, the 600-year-old Palace Museum receives between 6 to 8 million visitors from all over the world but mainly from China. People who work in the Forbidden City today have vastly different job descriptions than the workers of the Ming and Qing dynasties. Workers today keep the city clean and in good repair, take visitors on guided tours, work in the shops and cafés, and guard the valuable buildings and works of art. In addition to guides, cleaners, and security guards, many more people work in the various offices that have been set up within the city, including the Department of Antiquities, the Department of Paintings and Calligraphy, the Palace Department, and the Exhibition, Promotion, and Education Department.

Visitors can enjoy the city in various ways. Before actually reaching the Meridian Gate, there are several restaurants and a market outside, near

The Forbidden City was once a private and desolate place, but today it is densely populated with local and visiting people.

Tiananmen Square. At the City gates, people can stroll around, walking into the rooms and halls that are on display at their own leisure, or join a guided tour.

Today, in the Hall of Preserving Harmony, in the Outer Court, there is a café for everyone to enjoy. Years ago, this hall was used only by emperors and nobles for feasts on the evening of the Chinese New Year. The café today is busy but tastefully decorated, with no big signs or anything else that detracts from the site's atmosphere or the artifacts and original decorations around the walls and ceiling. Within the City are seven

A group of sumo wrestlers at the Forbidden City take a moment to relax.

galleries, including the Pottery Gallery, the Clock Gallery, the Treasure Gallery, and the Jade Gallery. Each gallery holds artifacts and works of art from the City's rich history.

Gigantic Portrait

For a small extra fee, visitors can climb the steps of the Gate of Heavenly Peace, or Tiananmen Gate, to look out over the great courtyard and see the panoramic view from which emperors inspected their armies or judged prisoners. A gigantic portrait of Mao Zedong has been hanging over this gate since 1949, along with two placards. One reads, "Long live the People's Republic

of China," and the other one reads, "Long live the great unity of the world's peoples." Today, on the western side of the Forbidden City, is a group of buildings. These buildings are the central headquarters of the Communist Party of China. They are a sign that the power of China's emperors is gone forever.

A portrait of Mao Zedong hangs over the Gate of Heavenly Peace, the entrance to the City.

Tales & Customs — Serving Heaven

The Gate of Supreme Harmony was one of the original buildings of the Ming city. The Ming called it the Gate of Serving Heaven. The Qing renamed it, along with many other buildings, to incorporate and emphasize their commitment to peace and harmony. This gate was the first working part of the Forbidden City. Protocol demanded that visitors enter the gate through the entrance appropriate to their rank. The gate is the place where emperors' wedding ceremonies were usually held.

CHAPTER 8 Preserving the Past

*S*ince the Forbidden City was first built for Emperor Yongle in 1420, maintenance and repair work on it has been near constant. However, in the years between 1911 and 1948—the years that covered the downfall of the Qing dynasty, World War I, and World War II—the Forbidden City fell into disrepair. Ongoing restoration and repair work in the City has taken place from the 1950s to the present.

Keeping the City clean was considered a top priority during the Ming and Qing dynasties. This also the case today.

Retirement Restoration

For nearly a century, one of the most opulent structures inside the Forbidden City sat decaying and unseen. It was the Palace of Peaceful Longevity, the retirement home of Emperor Qianlong, which he had built between 1771 and 1776. Out of respect for his grandfather, Kangxi, Qianlong chose to step down from the throne after nearly sixty years so as not to rule for longer than Kangxi, who had ruled for sixty-one years. At the age of eighty-four, Qianlong abdicated in favor of his son Jiaqing and lived happily in this palace, although he secretly continued to be involved in imperial affairs until his death three years later. Originally, this palace contained many richly decorated chambers, including a theater in which Chinese harps and violins were played and the Beijing Opera performed. It was surrounded by a four-courtyard garden in which Qianlong liked to sit and think in the evenings. To a certain extent, Qianlong had opened up China to the Western world. This was reflected in the objects in his retirement palace, which were a mixture of Qing dynasty decorations and Italian paintings that he greatly admired. The walls and ceilings were adorned with ornate wood carvings, jade, embroideries, and large paintings created by the Italian Jesuit missionary Giuseppe Castiglione. Today, a massive restoration project is set to return the palace to its former glory. But restorations are not always easy. For instance, the same materials used in ancient times are no longer available, and craftspeople who know the necessary techniques cannot always be found. These are problems that even modern technology cannot solve.

Many workers are employed in the Forbidden City to perform the constant repairs and maintenance required to preserve the City's magnificence.

Specialists are employed to restore delicate porcelain treasures.

A Symbol of Chinese History

In the early 1950s, great efforts were made to restore the Forbidden City to the magnificent and awe-inspiring place it had once been. Dirty and dilapidated halls and courts that lay under weeds and piles of garbage were cleared and cleaned. Crumbling walls were repaired and redecorated, and all buildings were fixed up with lighting, sprinkler systems, and security alarms. The moat, or Outer and Inner Golden Water, was dredged and cleaned. The Forbidden City is still the biggest complex of palaces in the world, and the Chinese government considers it one of the most important historical monuments in the country. Today, the Forbidden City—or Palace Museum, as it is now called— is under special care. A constant program of repair and restoration aims at bringing the buildings of the City back into the condition they were in when the Ming and Qing emperors lived and ruled in them.

Tales & Customs — The Jade Document

One ceremony that took place inside the Hall of Central Harmony was the updating and presentation to the emperor of the Qing family tree, known as the Jade Document. Three copies were made of the document: one to be housed in the Imperial Archives within the Forbidden City; one for the Clan Register Office in Beijing; and one for the Old Palace in Shenyang—the original center of Manchu power.

The Forbidden City

Almost every day, experts work on some area of the city, bringing it back to its former glory so visitors from China and around the world can marvel at it.

In the early 1980s, the Meridian Gate and some of the great ceremonial halls were restored. Several apartments were refurbished to their 19th-century state, while others were returned to the appearance they had during earlier periods. The renovations are extremely expensive and need the skills of many architects, historians, scientists, and other experts, but they are considered vital in order to allow people to see and

appreciate the past in all its splendor. Computers are being used to show how the buildings and interiors once looked and will look when restored. The repairs also help to revive some ancient skills and techniques that were practiced by the artists and craftspeople of imperial China that were being lost over time. There is now a reason for these skills and techniques to be

Many run-down houses near the Forbidden City in Beijing are being demolished and rebuilt as part of a plan to preserve historic sites. All historic sites and cultural relics are protected throughout the process.

Tales & Customs — Beijing Opera

The Beijing Opera often performed for the emperor. It consisted of the "internal troupe," which was made up of eunuchs, and the "external troupe," whose actors were specially selected to come and perform for the emperor and his family. The Beijing Opera is a unique form of opera, combining dance, acrobatics, and music. Its costumes, make-up, and gestures all have symbolic meanings that audiences of imperial China would have understood.

The Imperial Seals, held in the Hall of Union, are wrapped in plastic to protect them from damage.

new world of space and time . . . . [o]n the inner side of the gateway were to be observed palanquins bearing stately mandarins with ruby and coral 'buttons' and peacocks' feathers on their official hats and white cranes and golden pheasants on the front of their long outer garments of silk."

Although the Forbidden City has undergone many transformations throughout the centuries, stepping into the vast Outer Court is like stepping back several centuries into imperial China as it once was. Emperor Yongle might have been pleased to see that it remains an amazing example of the rich history of China— for all to see.

used, but training people in them and paying for their expertise is costly.

Seeing Through Twilight

The British official, scholar, and writer Reginald F. Johnson (1874–1938) served as a tutor and moral advisor to Puyi, the last emperor of China. He wrote about his experiences in a book called *Twilight in the Forbidden City* that was published in 1934. Through the vivid descriptions in this book of his life and surroundings in the Forbidden City, experts have been able to restore and renovate many of the decorations and buildings to their former appearance. In the following excerpt, Johnson describes his arrival in the Forbidden City and the costumes of the imperial court: "The imposing Gate of Spiritual Valor, through which I made my first entrance into the Forbidden City on March 3, 1919, led me to a

Temporary scaffolding was erected over one of the Forbidden City palaces during its renovation.

abdicated: gave up the role of king or queen to make way for another to take the throne.

ancestors: family members, usually those preceding grandparents, from whom a person is descended.

Anglo-Palladian: an 18th century architectural style combining the technique of 16th century Italian architect Andrea Palladio with English architectural styles.

artifacts: objects produced or shaped by human craft, especially objects remaining from earlier historical periods.

autocratic: related to rule by one leader who holds all the power over a country or state.

balustrades: ornamental railings or pillars of a building.

Buddhism: the religion and spiritual practices based on the teachings of Buddha, who believed that life is full of suffering caused by desire, that suffering ceases when desire ceases, and that enlightenment obtained through wisdom and meditation releases one from desire and suffering.

calligraphy: the art of beautiful, stylized, or elegant handwriting.

castrated: having had the male genitals surgically removed.

Communism: the political and economic system that aims to create a classless society in which all property is owned by the state, which is controlled by a single, unelected party.

concubine: a woman who lives with a man without being married to him, especially one who holds status in a household below the man's wife or wives.

contemplation: thoughtful observation or study.

corruption: dishonest or illegal behavior.

counterfeiting: the act of forging or imitating something, such as money, artworks, or documents.

courtiers: companions and advisors to the ruler of a nation.

crane: a type of long-necked bird.

dowager: an elderly woman of high social station who holds a title or property derived from her deceased husband.

dynasty: a succession of rulers belonging to the same family.

emperor: a male ruler of a political body that includes several nations.

enamel: a glasslike or semi-transparent hard coating applied to glass, pottery, and metal objects.

eunuch: a male servant who has been castrated.

exorcism: a ritual for the purpose of driving out an evil spirit.

famine: a severe food shortage.

feng shui: the Chinese belief that by positioning objects (such as buildings and furniture) in a way that is harmonious with patterns of yin and yang and the flow of chi, an increased amount of happiness and good things will result.

humidity: the amount of moisture in the atmosphere.

imperial: related to an empire.

incense: a substance that is burned for the sweet smell it produces.

Jesuit: a member of the Society of Jesus, a Roman Catholic order of priests.

Longevity: the length of a life.

Manchu: a member of a people native to Manchuria, who ruled China during the Qing dynasty.

Ming: the Chinese dynasty that lasted from 1368 to 1644, and was noted for its foreign trade, achievements in scholarship, and development of the arts, especially in porcelain, textiles, and painting.

missionary: a person who travels to promote his or her faith.

moat: a body of water surrounding a building, usually a castle or tower.

Mongol: a member of the traditionally nomadic (traveling) peoples of Mongolia.

movable type: a printing technology that uses movable raised letters that are fitted into grooves (in which they are formed into words), inked, and pressed onto paper.

nationalism: loyalty to a nation, especially accompanied by the view that one's nation is superior.

nobility: aristocracy, upper class.

North Star: the star located in the sky directly above the North Pole.

officials: people who have jobs in a government.

omens: signs that are believed to tell of future good or evil events.

opulent: showing great wealth.

pawned: lent in return for an amount of money.

Peking: the name given to the capital of China by French missionaries; this name was changed back to its correct name of Beijing in 1949 by the Communist Party of China.

philosophy: the study of knowledge, reality, ethics, and related issues.

phoenix: a mythical bird that died in a burst of flames and then rose again to life from the ashes.

porcelain: a light, smooth form of delicate white clay used to make ornaments and items such as plates and bowls.

portico: a porch or walkway with a roof supported by columns, often leading to the entrance of a building.

prosperity: success or good fortune.

prostrate: to lie face down.

protocol: an official procedure or pattern of behavior.

Qianlong: the Chinese emperor (1735–1796) of the Qing dynasty who subdued the Turkish and Mongolian threats to northern China, expanded the empire, and was a patron of the arts.

Qing: the Chinese dynasty that lasted from 1644 to 1912, during which Western influence and trade led to the Opium Wars (1839–1842) with Britain and the Boxer Rebellion (1898–1900), and which was China's last dynasty before the country was taken over by nationalist revolutionaries.

regent: a person appointed to lead a nation because the monarch is too young or unfit to rule.

relics: objects or beliefs from an earlier time.

republic: a state in which power is held by the people.

revolution: the overthrowing of a government by force.

scholar: a person who does research to develop specialized knowledge.

Taoism: a philosophical system that advocates living a simple, honest life and not interfering with the natural course of events.

tranquility: the state of being peaceful and free from disturbances.

tyrant: a brutal absolute ruler.

valor: courage in the face of danger.

yin and yang: the basic principles of nature in Chinese philosophy that are related to balance and harmony and that are linked to Feng Shui. Yin is the female, softer aspect of the world, and yang is the masculine, stronger aspect of the world. According to Chinese philosophy, a balance of yin and yang is needed in everything.

Yuan: the Chinese dynasty that lasted from 1279 to 1368 that was established by Mongolian ruler Kublai Khan.